Blaze the Trail, Snoopy

Charles M. Schulz

Selected cartoons from AND A WOODSTOCK
IN A BIRCH TREE Volume 2

CORONET BOOKS
Hodder and Stoughton

PEANUTS comic strips: Copyright © 1978 United Feature
Syndicate, Inc.

First published in the United States of
America 1981 by Fawcett Books

Coronet edition 1982

British Library C.I.P.

Schulz, Charles M.
    Blaze the trail, Snoopy.
    I. Title
    741.5'973

ISBN 0 340 28436 6

Printed and bound in Great Britain for
Hodder and Stoughton Paperbacks, a
division of Hodder and Stoughton Ltd.,
Mill Road, Dunton Green, Sevenoaks,
Kent (Editorial Office: 47 Bedford
Square, London, WC1 3DP) by
Cox & Wyman Ltd, Reading

**Also by the same author,
and available in Coronet Books:**

→

LAST WEEK MY MOTHER SAID TO ME, "EUDORA, I THINK YOU SHOULD GO TO SUMMER CAMP!"

SO HERE I AM IN THE WILDERNESS

IT'S NOT TOO BAD...YOU MAY EVEN LIKE IT...

SO I'LL ASK YOU THE SAME THING I ASKED HER...

WHAT IF I GET EATEN BY AN ANTELOPE?

SCHULZ

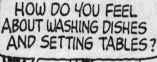

YOU'RE GOING TO TAKE ME FISHING? THAT'S GREAT! I DON'T KNOW ANYTHING ABOUT FISHING

WELL, WHAT WE'LL DO IS, WE'LL GO DOWN ON THE DOCK, AND SEE IF THERE ARE ANY FISH IN THE LAKE, AND THEN...

I SEE ONE!

YOU JUST PADDLE AROUND THERE AWHILE, AND I'LL EXPLAIN ABOUT THESE POLES...

OKAY, EUDORA, YOU FISH IN THIS PART OF THE STREAM, AND I'LL FISH DOWN THERE IN THAT PART...

I DON'T THINK THIS IS GOING TO WORK

WHAT'S THE TROUBLE?

EITHER THE STREAM IS TOO NARROW, OR MY LINE IS TOO LONG...

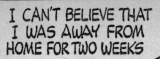

I CAN'T BELIEVE THAT I WAS AWAY FROM HOME FOR TWO WEEKS

I NEVER THOUGHT I'D MAKE IT... I THOUGHT I'D CRACK UP... INSTEAD, I FEEL AS THOUGH I'VE MATURED...

THERE'S YOUR MOTHER WAITING FOR YOU AT THE BUS STOP...

SO MUCH FOR MATURITY!

WHY DO DOGS SIT IN CARS, AND BARK?

I WAS JUST OVER IN THE PARKING LOT BY THE SUPERMARKET...

THERE WAS THIS DOG IN THE BACK OF A STATION WAGON, AND HE WAS BARKING AND BARKING AND BARKING

I'VE PLAYED AGAINST "CRYBABY" BOOBIE BEFORE! IT'S AN EXPERIENCE!

HER BROTHER, BOBBY BOOBIE, DOESN'T SAY MUCH, BUT SHE COMPLAINS ABOUT EVERYTHING

JUST DON'T LET HER GET TO YOU...JUST LET IT ALL GO IN ONE EAR AND OUT THE OTHER...

THAT'S THE SPIRIT, PARTNER!

ALL RIGHT, PARTNER, IT'S MATCH POINT...

WE HAVE TO CONCENTRATE! THAT'S THE SECRET, PARTNER! CONCENTRATE!

I GOT A LETTER FROM MY BROTHER, SPIKE, TODAY...

HAS ANYONE EVER NOTICED THAT THE PORTRAIT OF CARL SANDBURG ON A THIRTEEN-CENT STAMP LOOKS LIKE PANCHO GONZALES?

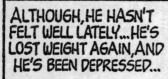

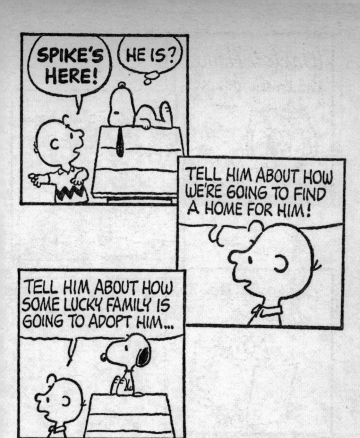

YES, WE'RE THE PARTY THAT RAN THE AD IN THE NEWSPAPER...

YES, WE'RE TRYING TO FIND A NICE HOME FOR A DOG..ACTUALLY, HE'S THE BROTHER OF OUR OWN DOG...

OH, NO...HE WOULDN'T BE A LOT OF TROUBLE... NO, HE AMUSES HIMSELF QUITE WELL...

AH, COLONEL HOGAN!

STILL HITTING BALLS WITH THE GARAGE, I SEE...

IT'S GOOD PRACTICE..HE GETS EVERYTHING BACK

I WAS SURPRISED YOU DIDN'T PLAY DOUBLES AT WIMBLEDON THIS YEAR..

THE GARAGE HATES TO FLY

JOE DI MAGGIO NEVER COMPLAINED ABOUT PLAYING BALL ON A HOT DAY!

WHO WAS JOE DI MAGGIO?

ONE OF THE GREATEST OUTFIELDERS WHO EVER LIVED, THAT'S WHO!

I THOUGHT HE JUST DRANK COFFEE

WELL, WE LOST AGAIN

LUCY, DO ME A FAVOR...

ASK OUR PLAYERS TO LINE UP TO SHAKE HANDS WITH THE OTHER TEAM AND SAY, "NICE GAME"

OKAY, TEAM, IT'S HYPOCRITE TIME!!

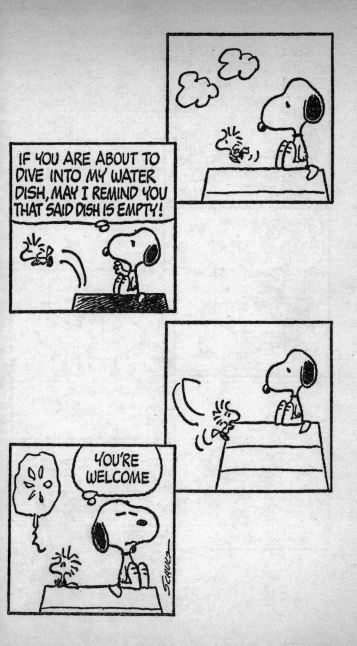

ALL RIGHT, TROOPS...
BEFORE WE GO ON OUR
HIKE, I'LL CALL THE ROLL

WOODSTOCK! CONRAD!
BILL! OLIVIER!

ZZZZ

I SHOULD NEVER
CALL THE ROLL
BEFORE NOON!

SCHULZ

DO YOU ALL SEE THAT HILL OVER THERE?

OUR OBJECTIVE TODAY IS TO CLIMB TO THE TOP OF THAT HILL...

ARE THERE ANY QUESTIONS?

NO, CONRAD, I DON'T KNOW WHAT THE MEANING OF LIFE IS!

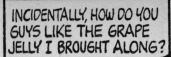

OKAY, MEN, THE HIKE IS OVER... WE'RE HOME!

THIS IS WHERE YOU LIVE...WAKE UP!

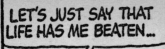

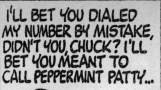

WHERE ARE YOU GOING, BIG BROTHER?

WELL, I FINALLY GOT UP NERVE TO CALL THAT LITTLE RED-HAIRED GIRL, BUT I DIALED MARCIE BY MISTAKE, AND GOT A DATE WITH PEPPERMINT PATTY...

I THINK YOU'RE TOO WISHY-WASHY, BIG BROTHER

IT'S NOT A LOST ART!

SCHOOL JUST STARTED AND ALREADY I SHOULD QUIT!

MY TEACHER YELLS AT ME, THE KIDS LAUGH AT ME AND THE PRINCIPAL HATES ME

WHAT ABOUT THE CUSTODIAN?

HE VACUUMED UP MY LUNCH!

YES, MA'AM? YOU WANT ME TO WORK OUT THE PROBLEM AT THE BOARD?

WELL, LET'S SEE.. WE HAVE THESE NUMBERS HERE, DON'T WE?

THESE ARE NICE NUMBERS, MA'AM..

➤

A FOUR, A SIX, A SEVEN, AN EIGHT, A FIVE AND A TWO

OH, YES, AND WE ALSO HAVE AN X ...

WELL, THE PROBLEM SEEMS TO BE TO TRY TO FIND OUT WHAT THIS X IS DOING AMONG ALL THESE NUMBERS...

IS HE AN OUT-SIDER? WAS HE INVITED TO JOIN THE GROUP? IT'S AN INTERESTING QUESTION...

LET'S FIND OUT WHAT THE REST OF THE CLASS THINKS... YOU THERE, IN THE THIRD ROW... WHAT DO YOU THINK ABOUT THIS? SPEAK UP!

MA'AM?

RATS! THREE MORE MINUTES AND THE BELL WOULD HAVE RUNG!

SCHULZ

Dear Grandma,
How are you? I am fine.

I have been working hard in school.

➤➤

PROBLEM NUMBER SIX...

"HOW MANY GALLONS OF CREAM CONTAINING 25% BUTTER FAT AND MILK CONTAINING 3½% BUTTER FAT MUST BE MIXED TO..

..OBTAIN 50 GALLONS OF CREAM CONTAINING 12½% BUTTER FAT?"

MA'AM, WOULD YOU SETTLE FOR TWENTY PUSH-UPS?

"A Guide to Running"

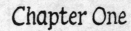

Chapter One

How to run like a rabbit.

Hop Hop Hop
Hop Hop Hop

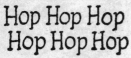

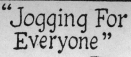

"Jogging For Everyone"

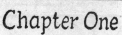

A Detailed Guide to Running

Chapter One

The Left Foot

WHAT ARE YOU EATING FOR LUNCH, EUDORA?

THIS IS A CHOCOLATE SANDWICH

I PUT A CHOCOLATE BAR BETWEEN TWO SLICES OF DARK BREAD

I OFTEN WONDER HOW IT WOULD TASTE WITH GRAVY ON IT...

EUDORA! WHAT ARE YOU DOING HERE? THERE'S NO SCHOOL ON SATURDAY!

THERE ISN'T? THAT EXPLAINS EVERYTHING...

SATURDAY'S THE ONLY DAY I NEVER GET ANYTHING WRONG

I WONDER IF IT'S TOO LATE TO BECOME A DISCO...

MORE FUN WITH PEANUTS FROM CORONET

CHARLES M. SCHULZ